Up In Space

A Counting Book

By Chris Lensch

Special thanks to the Longway Planetarium for taking the time to make sure I had my facts straight.   C.L.

8

First published by Experience Early Learning Company
7243 Scotchwood Lane, Grawn, Michigan 49637 USA

Text © 2015 by Experience Early Learning Co.
Printed and Bound in the USA

ISBN: 978-1-937954-20-8
visit us at www.ExperienceEarlyLearning.com

Up In Space

A Counting Book

By Chris Lensch

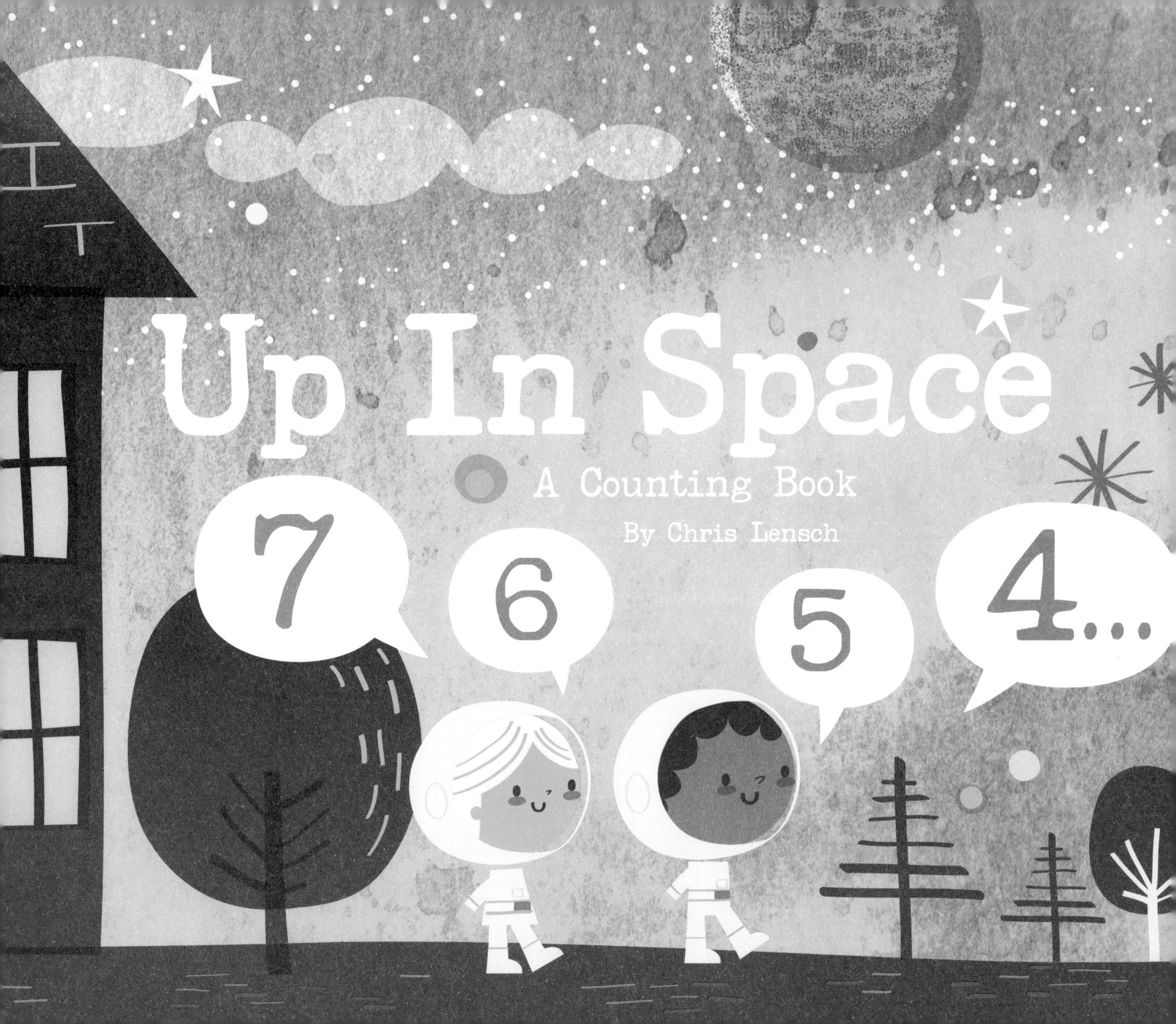

2

Blast

off!

Let's count

the planets

up in space,

and learn

some facts about

each place.

We will start at planet number one,
the planet closest to the sun.
As we see it come into sight,
it's hot all day and cold at night.

36 MILLION MILES FROM THE SUN

6

Mercury!

Planet number two hides in a cloud.
It's covered in an acid shroud.

9

All of these clouds trap in the heat;
it's the hottest planet we will meet!

67 MILLION MILES FROM THE SUN

10

Venus!

We think you'll like planet number three.
It's the only planet with a tree.

With food to eat and water to drink,
it's the best place to live, we think.

93 MILLION MILES FROM THE SUN

Earth!
(our home)

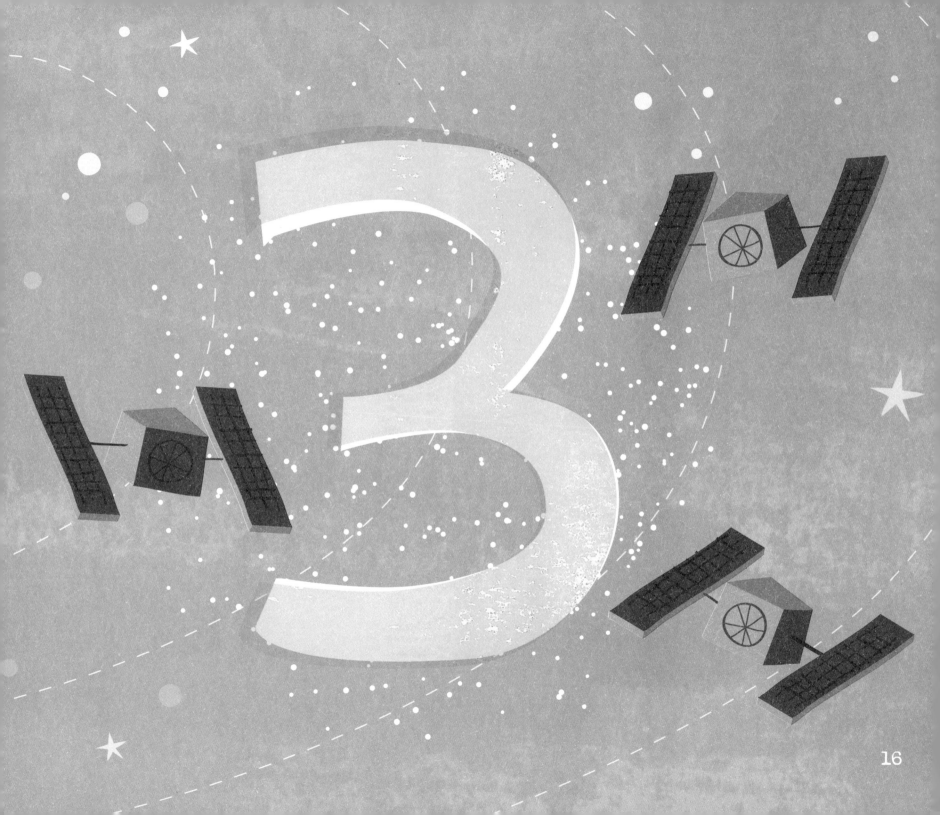

In space there is so much to explore, like the tallest mountain on planet number four.

But watch out for a stormy gust,
or you might get covered with red dust!

142 MILLION MILES FROM THE SUN

Mars!

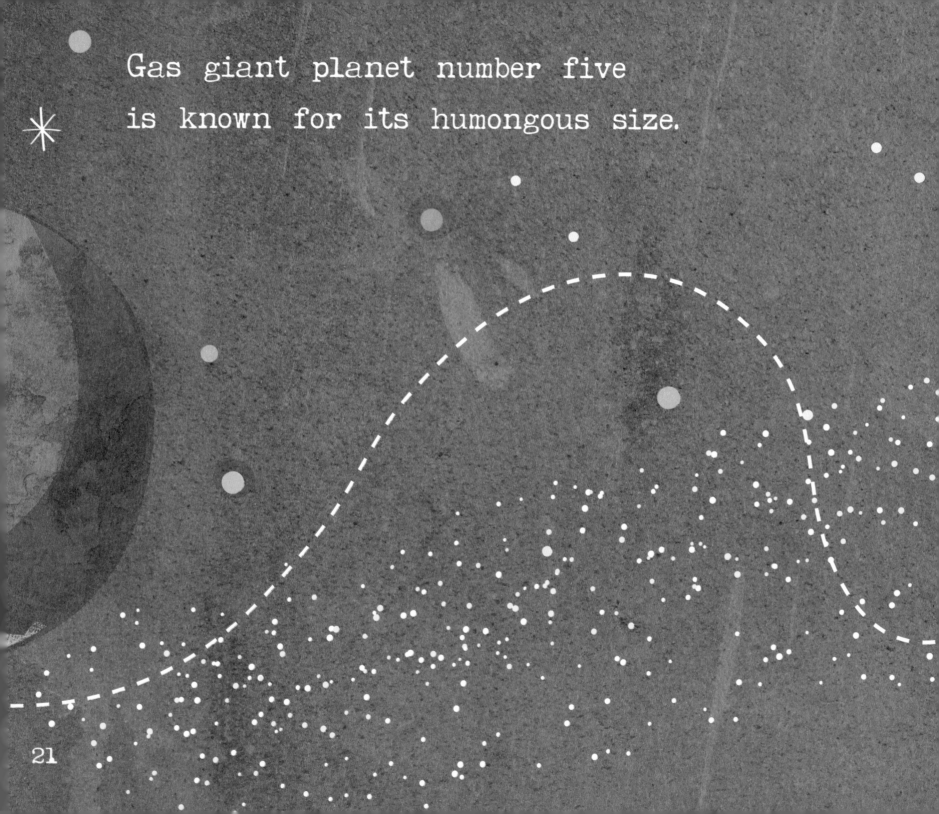

Gas giant planet number five
is known for its humongous size.

Look closely and you just might spot,
a storm that makes a big, red dot.

484 MILLION MILES FROM THE SUN

Jupiter!

23

Around planet number six is
a fancy thing:
spinning ice rocks make
a colorful ring.

And as for moons, there are sixty-two!
See if you can count a few!

Saturn!

Planet number seven takes the spot
as the coldest place that we will stop.

No other planet we have spied
spins around upon its side.

←---------- 1.8 BILLION MILES FROM THE SUN

Uranus!

Planet number eight, we are finally here.
A gassy, icy, windy sphere.

It takes 165 years to go around our sun while Earth takes 1 to get it done.

<----------- 2.8 BILLION MILES FROM THE SUN

Neptune!

A little further Pluto shines,
formerly planet number nine.

But scientists for now insist
we take it off the planet list.

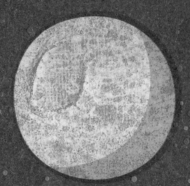

 3.6 BILLION MILES FROM THE SUN

That's it! We're done. We've seen them all,
from far and near to big and small.

It was so much fun, and you did great!
Let's count again from 1 to 8!

Mercury

Venus

Jupiter

Saturn

41

3

Earth

4

Mars

7

Uranus

8

Neptune

42

Our Solar System

The Sun

Mercury

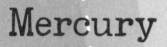

Venus

Earth

Satellite

Mars

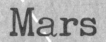

Asteroids

43

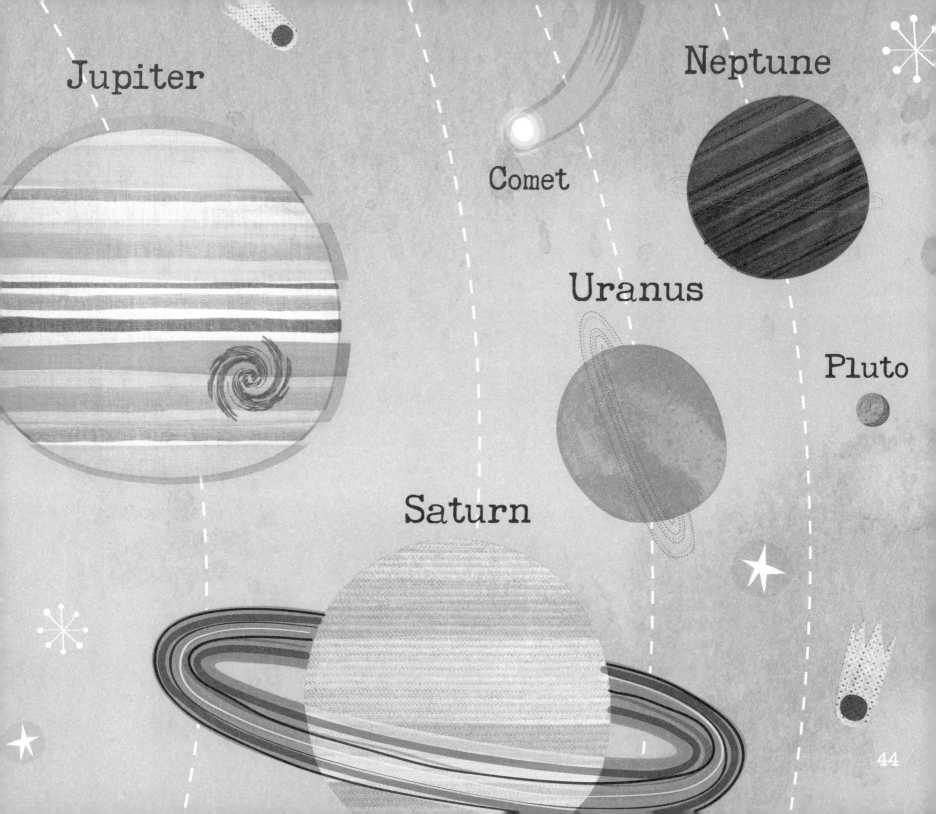

Jupiter

Comet

Neptune

Uranus

Pluto

Saturn

44

experience™
Early Learning

Experience Early Learning specializes in the development and publishing of research-based curriculum, books, music and authentic assessment tools for early childhood teachers and parents around the world. Our mission is to inspire children to experience learning through creative expression, play and open-ended discovery. We believe educational materials that invite children to participate with their whole self (mind, body and spirit) support on-going development and encourage children to become the authors of their own unique learning stories.

www.ExperienceEarlyLearning.com

45